The Professor's Book of First Names

"Sticks and stones will break my bones,
but names will never hurt me."
—*CHILDREN'S RHYME*

"As his name, so is he."
—*THE BIBLE*

"A name is sound and smoke."
—*GOETHE*

"How many Caesars and Pompeys . . . by mere
inspiration of the names, have been rendered worthy
of them? And how many . . . are there, who might
have done exceedingly well in the world, had not their
characteristics and spirits been totally depressed (by
their names)?"
—*STERNE*

"A rose by any other name would smell as sweet."
—*SHAKESPEARE*

"A good name is better than riches."
—*CERVANTES*

Thomas V. Busse, Ph.D.

The Professor's Book of First Names

The Green Ball Press
Elkins Park, Pennsylvania

Manufactured in the United States of America

Library of Congress Cataloging in Publication Data

Busse, Thomas V.
   The professor's book of first names.

   Bibliography: p.
   1. Names, Personal—Psychological aspects.
I. Title.
CS2377.B84 1984   929.4′4′019   83-80773
ISBN 0-9610950-0-8
ISBN 0-9610950-1-6 (pbk.)

For
Jeanne Lynn Busse
Michael Douglas Busse
Kathleen Kim Busse
Pauline Mary Busse

Contents

Table of Lists		11
1	Labeling	17
2	The Popularity of First Names	22
3	The Rise and Fall of Names	27
4	Choosing a Name	38
5	Choosing a Name: Bits and Pieces	45
6	Unusual Names	53
7	Nicknames	59
8	A Family of Nicknames	68
9	The Power of Names	71
10	Changing Your Name	77
11	Practical Questions	81
12	Intriguing Questions	87
Appendix A Popularity Ratings of Boys' Names		95
Appendix B Popularity Ratings of Girls' Names		99
Sources of Quotations		105
References		107
Articles and Papers on First Names by Professor Busse		117

Lists

1. Twenty Best Liked and Twenty Least Liked Boys' Names   23
2. Twenty Best Liked and Twenty Least Liked Girls' Names   24
3. Top Ten Names in New York City in 1898, 1928, 1948, and 1964   25
4. Ten Fast Rising Boys' Names   29
5. Ten Fast Falling Boys' Names   30
6. Ten Fast Rising Girls' Names   32
7. Ten Fast Falling Girls' Names   34
8. Persons Boys Are Named After   42
9. Persons Girls Are Named After   43
10. Popularity Ratings of Sexually-Ambivalent Names   49
11. Popularity Ratings of Girls' Double Names   51
12. Twenty Unusual American Boys' and Girls' Given Names   56
13. The Origins of Boys' Nicknames   60
14. The Origins of Girls' Nicknames   62
15. Nicknames Liked by Those Who Have Them   65
16. Nicknames Disliked by Those Who Have Them   66

11

Acknowledgments

I am grateful to my wife, Pauline Busse, for her help throughout the writing of this book. I also wish to express my appreciation to Suzanne Busse, Sandra Mangano, Richard S. Mansfield, and John Myers for their suggestions on earlier drafts. Finally, I must add a special note of thanks to my nine-year-old daughter, Jeanne, whose unflagging enthusiasm after reading every draft of every chapter inspired me to persevere.

About the Author

Professor Busse received his Ph.D. from the University of Chicago and currently teaches human development at Temple University. Dr. Busse was a Senior Fulbright Professor in the Department of Psychology at the University of Hamburg, West Germany, during the 1981-82 academic year. A licensed psychologist, he has published numerous articles and two previous books: *The Psychology of Creativity and Discovery* and *Activities in Child and Adolescent Development.*

Dr. Busse has been researching the psychology of first names for over fifteen years and has authored ten articles about names in such scholarly journals as *Psychology in the Schools*, the *Journal of Social Psychology,* and the *Journal of Psychology.*

The Professor's
Book of
First Names

1
Labeling

A name is a label. Names like Campbell Soup, Xerox, and Coca Cola represent great corporations and certify the quality of their products. Corporate slogans reinforce this link with presumed quality: "With a name like Smucker's, it has to be good." "Make sure. Make it Minute Maid." "Hershey. The great American chocolate bar." The current American craze for designer jeans carries labeling to an extreme. Otherwise sensible mothers pamper teenage daughters with extravagantly priced Jordache or Gloria Vanderbilt jeans.

In a similar way personal names represent us, and are therefore important to us. We can obtain boats, cars, and trips to Tahiti with only our signatures. Legal proceedings are apt to commence if our names are derogatorily mentioned in newspapers or magazines. Our tombstones are likely to be engraved with little more than our names.

These personal labels that are our names bear not only the sum of our own deeds, but also an inherited stock of associations. My name, Thomas

HAGAR THE HORRIBLE by Dik Browne. Reprinted by permission of King Features Syndicate, Inc.

V. Busse, or less formally Tom, is encrusted with connotations that are quite independent of my personal characteristics. My first name, Thomas, is stereotyped as conservative, large, soft, and cuddly. The shortened version, Tom, is much better liked than its longer parent. The middle initial, "V," conveys a measure of uniqueness and originality. The middle initial, "X," would do this even better. My use of a middle initial indicates a certain stiffness, formality, and status.

The last name, Busse, is of mixed French-German ancestry and generally communicates an image of one or the other. Many persons are unsure of its pronunciation. Some choose to award it a French accent: Buce (rhymes with the color puce); others use an English, Bus-see; a few use the German, Boos-seh. Americans find it a rather unusual name, one flavored with foreign implications. In French, Busse means simply "woods" or one who lived by the woods. It was interesting to observe my children's reactions to that fact: to be named Kathleen Woods, Michael Woods, or Jeanne Woods. It was as though a part of their uniqueness would be excised. My daughters may marry a Smith or Brown, but I doubt it.

Almost all first names have acquired commonly-accepted meanings that we call stereotypes. Some have developed over millennia; others are of recent origin. Judas has not been much in vogue since the crucifixion, Adolph may not recover for a thousand years, and Archie (a.k.a. Bunker) now turns us off. Parents when choosing a name, unconsciously or not, select the stereotypes they wish their children to bear. For example, the name, Shawn, carries stereotypes of Irish, quiet, shy, and timid. Stanley is viewed as an intellectual "nerd." Roger is dull and boring, average but honest.

Why do parents give children names like Stanley—names with generally negative stereotypes? The most important reason is that about 40% of girls and almost a majority of boys are named for someone very special to the parents. The name, Stanley, may not be that well liked by the parents either, but it would devastate Grandma Whyte if the benefits of her late husband's name were denied to her first grandson. It is also possible that the stereotypes associated with "Stanley" have changed since grandfather's birth 52 years ago. Such shifts are fairly common for girls' names, but relatively infrequent for boys' names.

The stereotypes associated with our names may be ill-suited to the images we have or wish to have of ourselves. We may feel impelled to change our names with the hope that our identities will be similarly altered. A surprising number of persons have, without legalities or fanfare, assumed a new first name (Margaret became Sue when she left for college), or replaced an undesired first name with a middle one. A smaller number have petitioned to legally change their names: Ralph Pyrzkus became Michael Page, shedding at once both a first name of falling popularity and a difficult to pronounce, foreign-sounding surname. Other name changes are not so voluntary: a woman generally takes the last name and to an extent the identity of her husband. Assuming the name of the rich banker's son from up on the hill can markedly improve the courtesy and service extended to a young woman by the town merchants.

Stereotyping on the basis of first names is only one of many stereotypings that influence us. Ethnicity, race, eyeglasses, stature, hair color, and facial attractiveness also produce stereotyped expectations in the mind of the beholder. But since many psychological studies show that names do influence their bearers, it is sensible to carefully choose the names of our children. Moreover, our own names may deserve a second thought and, subsequently, a second choice.

2
The Popularity of First Names

A rose by any other name would smell as sweet.

Maybe Shakespeare was right about roses, but he was wrong about people. In this highly mobile, media-oriented country, superficial personal characteristics such as first names count, particularly in making that important first impression in a job interview or on a date.

Recently I asked about 300 high school seniors to rate the popularity of 246 girls' names and 179 boys' names. Their ratings are presented in Appendix A for boys' names and Appendix B for girls' names. The twenty best liked and twenty least liked boys' and girls' names can be found in Lists 1 and 2.

Lists of the ten names given most frequently to babies in New York City have been published for 1898, 1928, 1948, and 1964. A comparison of these four lists with current popularity ratings from my research is instructive. Of today's 20 best liked boys' names, 10 are included in the New York City lists. John and Joseph appear on all four, while

List 1
Twenty Best Liked and Twenty
Least Liked Boys' Names

Best Liked	*Least Liked*
1. Michael	1. Schuyler
2. David	2. Bela
3. Mark	3. Florian
4. Anthony	4. Bartholomew
5. Daniel	5. Khalig
6. Stephen	6. Lyman
7. John	7. Malig
8. Brian	8. Altair
9. Scott	9. Sumner
10. Christopher	10. Rajiv
11. Keith	11. Armin
12. Joseph	12. Ingmar
13. Thomas	13. Grier
14. Kevin	14. Faber
15. Jonathan	15. Tracey
16. Gary	16. Melvin
17. Eric	17. Ford
18. James	18. Harvey
19. Robert	19. Alfred
20. Andrew	20. Herbert

List 2
Twenty Best Liked and Twenty
Least Liked Girls' Names

Best Liked	*Least Liked*
1. Michelle	1. Watonah
2. Jill	2. Lola May
3. Jacqueline	3. Edith
4. Jennifer	4. Shobhana
5. Cheryl	5. Rosemede
6. Suzanne	6. Bernice
7. Dawn	7. Ella Mae
8. Kristi	8. Temperance
9. Andrea	9. Towanda
10. Nancy	10. Meta
11. Susan	11. Mary Helen
12. Nicole	12. Myra
13. Karen	13. Wanda
14. Danielle	14. Bonita
15. Lisa	15. Dorothea
16. Robin	16. Jeri Ann
17. Dana	17. Isabella
18. Stephanie	18. Felica
19. Christina	19. Lucinda
20. Linda	20. Eveann

List 3
Top Ten Names in New York City

1898	1928	1948	1964
		BOYS	
John	John	Robert	Michael
William	William	John	John
Charles	Joseph	James	Robert
George	James	Michael	David
Joseph	Richard	William	Steven
Edward	Edward	Richard	Anthony
James	Robert	Joseph	William
Louis	Thomas	Thomas	Joseph
Francis	George	Stephen	Thomas
Samuel	Louis	David	Tie { Richard / Christopher
		GIRLS	
Mary	Mary	Linda	Lisa
Catherine	Marie	Mary	Deborah
Margaret	Annie	Barbara	Mary
Annie	Margaret	Patricia	Susan
Rose	Catherine	Susan	Maria
Marie	Gloria	Kathleen	Elizabeth
Esther	Helen	Carol	Donna
Sarah	Teresa	Nancy	Barbara
Frances	Jean	Margaret	Patricia
Ida	Barbara	Diane	Tie { Ann (e) / Theresa

James, Robert, Thomas, Michael, Stephen, David, Anthony,. and Christopher occur on at least one.

Fickle is the public's taste in girls' names. None of today's twenty best liked names were present on the New York City lists until Nancy, Susan, and Linda appeared in 1948. Lisa and Susan alone made the 1964 list. Thus only four of the 20 currently best liked girls' names previously appeared on the New York City lists.

Of the 20 least liked boys' and girls' names, none appeared on any of the four New York City lists: Popular names may fall from grace, but, within a lifetime, they are unlikely to end up in the pit reserved for the most disliked.

"Foreign" male names are generally disliked. However popular Ingmar might be in Sweden, Rocco in Italy, or Rajiv in India, they are losers here. In contrast, two of the most popular girls' names—Danielle and Nicole—are recent imports from abroad. This difference is consistent with the greater tolerance Americans show toward unusual girls' names.

3
The Rise and Fall
of Names

Great grandmother may have been named Rose, Lily, Violet, or Daisy. If not, perhaps Faith, Hope, Patience, or Prudence. Names gone with the bustle and the high wheeler.

But why? To find out I compared ratings of name popularity done in 1970 with similar ratings done in 1980 in the same school district. From 179 boys' names and 246 girls' names I selected the 10 names of each sex which had risen most and the 10 names which had declined most in popularity. Then I asked university students of varying ages (19–59 years) to write down "the associations that come to mind" for each of these 40 names. It was explained that such associations might include, for example, persons, places, and events. The names were presented in a random fashion, but boys' and girls' names were separated.

You might think that only gibberish would result because each of us knows different Jacquelines, Georges, and Bettys. But, although some name stereotypes are traceable to friends, acquaintances, and relatives, most are broadly held, even by individuals who have never known a Heather or a Cameron.

When large numbers of people are asked to freely associate to first names, individual perceptions (based, for example, on the George and Jacqueline who live down the street) cancel out. The commonly held stereotypes emerge. Lists 4, 5, 6, and 7 present these stereotypes.

Why have some names risen and others fallen so dramatically over the period from 1970 to 1980? Familiar persons or characters associated with a name provide clues. The fast-rising Nicholas is stereotyped as "Russian, cute, smart, and adorable." Viewers, especially female viewers, watching "Eight is Enough" would probably agree that the young Bradford boy, Nicholas, seems cute, smart, and adorable. This long-running TV show has influenced our perceptions of Nicholas.

Another example of an immensely popular TV show shaping a name stereotype can be found in Carroll O'Connor's portrayal of Archie on "All in the Family" and later "Archie Bunker's Place." In a similar way several generations of television Ralphs including Jackie Gleason's loud-mouthed, obnoxious Ralph Kramden in the "Honeymooners" and "Ralph the Mouth" on "Happy Days" have not helped Ralph's image.

Several girls' names have been especially influenced by ABC-TV's Soap Opera, "General

List 4
Ten Fast Rising Boys' Names

Name	Current Stereotype	Person or Character Most Associated with this Name
1. Cameron	a. Rich, snobbish, upper-class, sophisticated b. Westerner, cowboy	a. John Cameron Swazey b. Cameron Mitchell
2. Nathaniel	Traditional, proper, studious, intelligent	Nathaniel Hawthorne
3. Nicholas	Russian, cute, smart, adorable	a. Nicholas Bradford (From "Eight is Enough") b. Saint Nicholas c. Santa Claus d. Russian Czar
4. Shawn	Irish, quiet, shy, timid	Shawn Cassidy
5. Aubrey	Feminine, beautiful, attractive	None
6. Joel	Nice, friendly, childlike, Jewish	a. Joel Gray b. Billy Joel
7. Ian	Intelligent, foreign, British	a. Ian Fleming b. Ian Anderson
8. Nunzio	Italian/Spanish, mafia member	None
9. Dwayne	Black, unsophisticated, effeminate	None
10. Nathan	Jewish, huge, old	Nathan Hale

List 5
Ten Fast Falling Boys' Names

Name	*Current Stereotype*	*Person or Character Most Associated with this Name*
1. Archie	Funny, a bungler	a. Archie Bunker b. Archie (From comics and TV cartoon)
2. Skipper	Athletic, preppie	Skipper (From "Gilligan's Island" TV show)
3. Tracey	Feminine	Dick Tracy (Comic strip)
4. Ralph	Mediocre, working class, goofy, troublemaker	a. Ralph Nader b. Ralph Kramden (From "Jackie Gleason Show") c. Ralph the Mouth (From "Happy Days")
5. Dennis	Mischievous, Irish	Dennis the Menace (Comic Strip and TV show)

List 5
Ten Fast Falling Boys' Names *(continued)*

Name	Current Stereotype	Person or Character Most Associated with this Name
6. George	Regular guy, solid, dull, square	George Washington
7. Stanley	Intellectual, nerd, Polish	None
8. Jefferson	Black, intelligent	a. Thomas Jefferson b. George Jefferson (From "The Jeffersons" TV show)
Tie 9. Earl	a. Dumb, jock, Black b. English, nobility	Earl "the Pearl" Monroe (Basketball player)
Roger	Dull, boring, average, honest	a. Roger the Dodger b. Roy Rogers

List 6
Ten Fast Rising Girls' Names

Name	Current Stereotype	Person or Character Most Associated with this Name
1. Danielle	Beautiful, young, petite, intelligent, French	None
2. Nicole	French, ~~beautiful~~, ~~bright~~, spoiled	None
3. Jacqueline	Rich, sophisticated, formal, snobbish, attractive	a. Jacqueline Kennedy Onassis b. Jacqueline Susann
4. Birgit	Scandinavian/ German, sexy, strange, unusual	Bridgit Bardot (Perhaps she is associated with the name Birgit because of the foreign connotation of Birgit)
5. Dana	Athletic, unconventional, energetic	Dana Andrews (He is a man!)

List 6
Ten Fast Rising Girls' Names *(continued)*

Name	Current Stereotype	Person or Character Most Associated with this Name
6. Tara	Beautiful, elegant, conceited, Southerner	Tara Martin (From "All My Children" TV show)
7. Heather	Pretty, blond, bitchy	Heather Webber (From "General Hospital" TV show)
8. Leta	Unusual, foreign, strange	None
9. Vanessa	Elegant, distinguished, stuck up	Vanessa Redgrave
10. Monika	German, pretty, snob	Monica Quartermaine (From "General Hospital" TV show)

List 7
Ten Fast Falling Girls' Names

Name	Current Stereotype	Person or Character Most Associated with this Name
1. Penny	Cute, red-haired	None
2. Martha	Old, fat, hard-working	a. Martha Washington b. Martha Raye
3. Betty	Average, domestic, old-fashioned, typical housewife	Betty Boop (TV cartoon)
4. Brenda	None	a. Brenda Starr (Comic Strip) b. Brenda Vaccaro
5. Peggy	Average, typical	a. Peggy Fleming b. Peggy Lee
6. Bonnie	Cute, pretty	Bonnie (From "Bonnie and Clyde")

List 7
Ten Fast Falling Girls' Names *(continued)*

Name	Current Stereotype	Person or Character Most Associated with this Name
7. Mary Jo	Southerner, country girl, athletic, tomboy	Mary Jo Kopechne (Killed at Chappaquidick)
8. Wanda	Black, lower-class, unattractive	Wanda the Wicked Witch (From "Sesame Street" TV show)
9. Bunny	a. Preppie b. Dumb, blond, cute, immature	None
10. Jane	Plain, dull, ordinary	a. Jane Doe b. Jane (From Dick and Jane Beginning Readers) c. Jane (and Tarzan)

Hospital." The name, Heather, for example, is stereotyped as "pretty, blond, and bitchy." It is no coincidence that General Hospital's Heather Webber exemplifies similar characteristics.

Comic books and newspaper funnies have also contributed. Archie (of Archie, Veronica, Jughead and Company) has no doubt influenced perceptions of his name and may even have been instrumental in its selection for the Bunker character. Dennis' connotation as mischievous almost certainly owes a debt to the newspaper cartoon drawn by Hank Ketcham. And the name Brenda often brings to mind reporter Brenda Starr of comic strip fame.

Current media personalities may alter our view of names. Imagine a poor, unsophisticated, informal, and ugly Jacqueline? And Ms. Redgrave seems to have single-handedly shaped Vanessa as elegant, distinguished, and stuck up. After all, how many of us are acquainted with another Vanessa?

Movies have played a part in creating name stereotypes. Who can think of Tara without images of that beloved plantation in "Gone with the Wind"? Who can consider Bonnie without some thought to Clyde?

Sports figures too can shape the meaning of a name. In Philadelphia, Earl suggests the famous 76er guard, Earl "the Pearl" Monroe. Babe and

Reggie also bring forth images of athletic greatness.

These contemporary influences act against a background of long-established name stereotypes. For example, great men and women from the past continue to shape the images of some first names. Nathaniels are expected to be traditional, proper, studious and intelligent, reflecting our memory of that New England author of "The House of Seven Gables." Georges should be solid and square as we recall our first president.

4
Choosing a Name

Some cultures have restricted the freedom of parents to name their children. The Nazi government in Germany limited Jewish parents to Old Testament names (for example, Esau, Isaac, Rachel, Zipora), "Aryan" parents to "true" Germanic names (for example, Rudolf, Rainer, Hedwig, Gisela), and others to names that were neither Jewish nor "Aryan." Through these name decrees the Nazis caused additional difficulties for Jews and other minority members who wished to blend into the dominant national group. Distinct names also facilitated discriminatory treatment against Jews, Gypsies and others.

In America there are very few legal restrictions on choosing first names. Several years ago in Pennsylvania, for example, one boy was named Kook and another Zucchini. A girl was named Revolution.

The choice of names has sometimes been limited by long-established cultural patterns. For example, Ashanti children of West Africa are

BROOM HILDA by Russell Myers. Reprinted by permission of Tribune Company Syndicate, Inc.

named for the day of the week on which they are born. These "day names" differ for boys and girls. A boy born on Monday is named Kwadwo; and a girl, Adwoa. A boy born on Saturday bears the name, Kwame; a girl, Amma. Thus the former leader of Ghana, Kwame Nkrumah, was born on a Saturday.

In many areas of the world children are named for their relatives. Groups as diverse as American Jews, the Yakima Indians of Washington State, and the Maharashtra people of India customarily name children after deceased relatives. Greek tradition generally requires that the first son be named for the paternal grandfather and the first daughter after the paternal grandmother. The next boy and girl are named for the maternal grandparents. Icelanders often name their sons for a paternal grandfather.

Many peoples—for example, the Mashona of Zimbabwe and the Saramaka Maroons of Surinam—occasionally use names to commemorate events occurring at the time of birth. A severe rainstorm or a successful hunt may be commemorated in a child's name. This naming custom is rarely followed by Americans. One sometimes hears, however, of a baby named for an exceedingly violent coastal hurricane. And many a Victoria and Vickie were named to celebrate the American triumphs in 1945.

Other societies have allowed the children

themselves to participate in choosing their names. Among the Maori of New Zealand, the child to be named is read a long list of ancestral names. The name being read when the child sneezes is given to him/her as sneezing is believed to be a manifestation of the spirits. The Malays, too, allow a child to choose. A parent recites a list of names until the child smiles, this smile signifying the child's choice. Among the Dayaks of Borneo the child is allowed to grasp one of a group of small sticks upon which names have been inscribed.

In the United States parents choose children's names for varied reasons: The name has a pleasant sound; it compliments their last name; it brings forth pleasing associations or stereotypes. Many parents choose a name because a relative has previously borne it.

To explore American practices in more detail I polled several hundred American high school seniors about the origins of their names. A breakdown of their answers can be found in Lists 8 and 9.

Forty nine percent of the boys and 38 percent of the girls reported being named after someone. Fathers, grandfathers, and great grandfathers together constitute about 75 percent of all persons for whom boys are named. In contrast, a much smaller percentage of girls are named for their mothers, grandmothers, and great grandmothers.

Naming a child after a relative may create an

List 8
Persons Boys are Named After

Father	23%
Grandfather	11
Great-grandfather	5
Uncle	4
Mother	2
Great-uncle	1
Great-grandmother	1
Friend of parents	1
Favorite saint	1
Not named for someone	51%

List 9
Persons Girls Are Named After

Grandmother	7%
Mother	6
Miscellaneous relatives	5
Aunt	3
Friend of parents	3
Miscellaneous non-relatives	3
Father	2
Cousin	2
Great-aunt	2
Grandfather	1
Godmother	1
Great-grandmother	1
Favorite saint	1
Popular female singer	1
Not named for someone	62%

emotional bond between the older person and his/her namesake. Kin-naming can thus be used to strengthen an already strong bond with a favorite grandparent, uncle, or aunt. Or it can be used as a painless way to ease stressful relations with one or another grandparent. Hope of inheriting Great-Aunt Elizabeth's fortune would, of course, never intrude in discussions about possible names!

Incidentally, first born sons and daughters are, according to research by sociologist Alice Rossi, two to three times as likely to be named after a relative as are fourth and later born children.

If you plan to name a child after a favorite relative, proceed with caution. Many names that were heavy winners in your parents' or grand-parents' day are now liabilities. If you pin a Margaret, Frances, or Helen on your daughter, at least give her a popular middle name to which she can retreat in adolescence. A milder warning is appropriate when choosing a name for your son because boys' names shift in popularity at a slower pace than do girls' names. Remember though, school teachers and Army sergeants—to name two villains—have resurrected many a detested and long buried given name.

5
Choosing a Name: Bits and Pieces

This chapter treats a number of concerns: (1) junior names, (2) opposite sex and ambivalent names, (3) alliterative names, and (4) double names.

JUNIORS

The phenomenon of naming children after their parents has sometimes generated hostility in the offspring. For example, Henry James disliked his junior status intensely:

> I have a right to speak of that appendage—I carried it about for forty years . . . disliking it all the while, and with my dislike never in the least understood or my state pitied.

Children named for their parents are sometimes pushed to meet high parental expectations. Joseph P. Kennedy, Jr., John's older brother, was groomed by his father to be president.

High parental expectations are not reserved for identically-named children, but this naming practice may accentuate the pressures they receive. The identification of a boy with his father or a girl with her mother is a normal and desirable process. But if the standards are too high, or the pressure is too great, the child will suffer from futile attempts to realize the parent's dream. Low self-esteem is the logical outcome.

The objectionable effects of identical naming seem to fall most heavily on boys, probably because employment-related achievement pressures are focused more strongly on males.

Junior naming can also cause confusion. For example, one woman wrote to newspaper columnist Ann Landers:

> My oldest brother's name is George. At family gatherings, everyone goes crazy trying to figure out which George. There is Grandpa George, George Jr. (my father), and brother George and his son—also George. Of course, the kids called my brother Georgie Porgie all through grade school. In high school he became King George III. His son is "Jor-Four."

Most families accommodate by using different names, at least within the family circle. The father may be called John, and the boy, Johnny, Junior, Sonny, Chip, or some other nickname.

SEX AND NAMES

Not all children are given sex-appropriate names. Some years ago Johnny Cash sang of a young boy named Sue who had to fight to prove his masculinity. Names given to Pennsylvania babies in a recent year included boys named Sharon, Angela, Heather, and Jennifer, as well as girls named John, Douglas, Albert, and Nathan. Clerical errors may be responsible for some of these oddities, but Michael Learned, who played the mother on "The Waltons" television show, bears witness that some women do carry men's names.

Sometimes parents, in desperation for a son, may give a boy's name to their daughter—for example, Walter, George, or Richard. These names, customarily given to boys, are almost certain to provoke taunting and teasing. Or, disappointed at the birth of a son, parents may give the lad a girl's name. A close friend of my father endured the name Mary for nineteen years before legally changing it to Michael. Other similarly dissatisfied parents may choose a sexually-ambivalent name like Robin or Terry.

Sexually ambivalent names—such as Aubrey, Shelley, or Carroll—are entwined with feminine connotations. For example, psychologists James Bruning and William Albott asked college students to assign first names to men's photographs. A man who appeared strong and virile was labeled names such as Bart or Mac, while a placid-faced male was tagged Shelley or Carroll. These feminine name connotations should be easily overcome by All-American-Boy types, but if the lad is slight of build, non-athletic, and bookish, the combination

Reprinted by permission of Mrs. Helen L. Baldwin.

List 10
Popularity Ratings of
Sexually Ambivalent Names

Name	Rated as a Boys' Name	Rated as a Girls' Name
Dana	4	10
Francis/Frances	5	3
Lee	8	7
Robin	4	10
Terry	8	9
Tracey/Tracy	1	8

Rated on a scale from 1 to 10.
Ratings 9 and 10 indicate well-liked names.
Ratings 3 through 8 signify average popularity.
Ratings 1 and 2 indicate disliked names.

may be too much. Rejection and possibly ridicule by his male schoolmates are likely to result.

List 10 contains the popularity ratings of six ambivalent names taken from my research. Five names—Dana, Francis, Lee, Robin, and Terry— were rated about average as boys' names. One— Tracey—was disliked as a boys' name. Danas, Robins, and Traceys fared much better as girls' names than as boys' names.

ALLITERATIVE NAMES

Dana had three older sisters: Dorothy, Doris, and Deanna. Her father often joked "that they had about run out of girls' names beginning with D and if they had had another girl, he'd have said 'Damnation' and she would have been called that." Other parents remain delighted with alliterative naming. For example, Joseph and Jean, the parents of a large Catholic Midwestern family, named their children: Joan, Jerry, Joseph, Judy, Jeffrey, Janet, John, and James.

The establishing of patterns for children's names is an ancient custom. In ninth century England, Alfred the Great christened his offspring: Ethelflaed, Edward, Edmund, Ethelgifu, Aelfth- ryth, and Ethelweard.

Parents also sometimes select rhyming names—Barry, Kerry, Mary, and Sherry, or ones

List 11
Popularity Ratings of Girls' Double Names

Name	Rating
Suzanne	10
Joanne	9
Marianne	7
Rosemary	6
Rosemarie	6
Rose Ann	5
Mary Ellen	5
Mary Elizabeth	3
Beth Ann	3
Mary Lynn	3
Mary Kay	2
Mary Jo	2
Doranne	2
Lou Ann	2
Jeri Ann	1
Mary Helen	1
Ella Mae	1
Lola May	1

Rated on a scale from 1 to 10.
Ratings 9 and 10 indicate well-liked names.
Ratings 3 through 8 signify average popularity.
Ratings 1 and 2 indicate disliked names.

devoted to a theme—Hope, Joy, Patience, and Prudence.

The linking of children's names is innocuous so long as some weird name isn't picked in order to suit a predetermined pattern. What do you name the fourth girl after April, May, and June?

DOUBLE NAMES

In the American South children are frequently given a two-part name—George Robert or Rose Ann, for example. Compound names—Marianne, Rosemary—are used throughout this land. Girls' double names of both types were rated for popularity in my research. Boys' double names are scarce in the Philadelphia region, and none were included. The ratings of six compound and twelve two-part girls' names are presented in List 11.

The two-part names are often disliked. Four—Jeri Ann, Mary Helen, Ella Mae, and Lola May—are highly disliked.

Mary is more popular than any of its six two-part names. Even combinations involving more desirable names—Ellen and Lynn—show lower ratings than Mary alone. Two-part names are distinctly out of fashion in the Northeast.

Compound names do not share the disliked status of two-part names. One, Suzanne, is very well liked, influenced possibly by the haunting ballad sung by Judy Collins.

6
Unusual Names

The national media recently spotlighted some of my name research which showed that persons with liked names, especially girls, generally had higher achievement and IQ scores than those with disliked names. Lists of liked and disliked names usually accompanied these findings. The disliked list disturbed some people.

I heard from Faber who attributed part of his business success to the uniqueness of his name. He wrote that Faber was remembered in a business world crowded with Toms, Dicks, and Harrys. Another correspondent, a woman named Margaret, abandoned her name after experiencing a class with eight other Margarets. Her middle name, Winifred, she wrote, lends her a "certain cachét." These testimonials suggest that there are people out there who love their—pick one—weird, creative, adventurous, uncommon, unique names.

Faber and Winifred's contentions are supported by an Ohio psychologist, James Bruning, who found that a disliked name, Cecil, embedded in a list of liked names was learned more quickly than the liked names. Singer Engelbert Humperdinck took advantage of this phenomenon. But rock groups—Grateful Dead, The Byrds, Kiss—have now selected unusual names with such predictability that the "Cecil" effect no longer works for them.

Consider also Bambi Tascarella, a technical assistant at NBC television. Hers is one of the dozens of names that rush by following the evening news when the news has been slow, and air time remains to be filled. One day a Sioux City, Iowa man noticed her name. He was struck by its uniqueness. He talked to his friends and together they started a Bambi Tascarella fan club. Swiftly there were members in New York, Chicago, and Los Angeles. Even David Brinkley indicated he would like to join.

Girls are more likely than boys to be given unusual names. This is reflected in the greater variety of names possessed by girls. In one sample of about 1700 elementary school children, I found 179 distinct boys' names, but 246 different girls' names. Names that were pronounced the same were considered identical even though they might be spelled differently. The ten most frequently occurring boys' names accounted for 40 percent of all boys' names, while for girls the corresponding figure was only 24 percent.

Unusual names come in many varieties. In List 12 I have assembled some actual names given to Americans. Boys have been named everything from Maverick—I wonder if his parents believed in self-fulfilling prophecies—to Haley's Comet and War Baby. Girls have been blessed with Equal Rights Amendment, Lonely, and Lucy Never Seen Joe, named because her father died before she was born.

Downright cruel names are sometimes given to children, names such as Kook, Bother, Nauseous, and Void. Perhaps mothers choose these names to retaliate for the pain of childbearing and delivery.

Psychologists have studied the effects of unusual names on their bearers. Several researchers have found that males with unusual names are more likely to be neurotic or psychotic. On the other hand, unusual names can be helpful under certain conditions. For example, members of the upper class who bear unusual names are more likely to be listed in *Who's Who*. An unusual name may cause particular individuals to set themselves apart and think of themselves as special: the same fire that destroys wood, purifies steel.

My research shows that some infrequently occurring names are well liked, and that some common names receive only slightly above average popularity ratings. The obvious solution is to

List 12
Twenty Unusual American Boys' and Girls' Given Names

Boys	Girls
Chastisement	Alpha Omega
Early Bird	Canless
Fury	Clendolia
Halley's Comet	Easter Glory
Indiana River	Equal Rights Amendment
Jesus-Christ-Came-Into-The-World-to-Save	Honthalena
	Icy Blizzard
Maverick	Kotex
McGeorge	Lonely
Pleasant Smiley	Lucy Never Seen Joe
Prezell	Margorilla
Matthew Mark Luke John	Merry Christmas
Self Rising	Mountain Bird
St. John	Nauseous
Sunday Night Supper	Oleomargarine
Theophilus	Rizpah
U.L.	Sweet Blossom
Vermont Connecticut	Thyomia
Void	Vendetta
War Baby	Venus
X.Y.Z.	

CROCK by Bill Rechin and Brant Parker. © 1977 Field Enterprises, Inc. Courtesy of Field Newspaper Syndicate

give your child an uncommon first name that everyone likes immensely. Unfortunately, other parents will probably have the same idea, and soon the name will be as common as dandelions. Danielle and Nicole are currently experiencing this popularity surge.

7
Nicknames

All my life I have been called Shorty by people.
I told one man my name was not Shorty and he
said I looked short. I told him he looked like
an idiot, but I hated to call him Idiot.

A frustrated and angry man wrote that letter.
He added that whenever someone called him
Shorty, it ruined his day, every time. He touched
familiar ground. Most of us know someone with a
derogatory or demeaning nickname—Wart, Cack-
le, Elephant, Squirt, or Bent.

Nicknames are given to persons in addition to
their legal given names. Customary short forms of
names—Jim, Tom, Dick—and "ee" names—Jimmy, Tommy, Dicky—are not, strictly speaking,
nicknames.

I questioned several hundred high school
seniors about their nicknames. Did they have
nicknames? If so, what were they? Why were these
nicknames given? Who uses them?

Fifty-five percent of the boys and 40 percent of
the girls reported having a nickname. In Lists 13
and 14 you can peruse the origins of these nick-

List 13
The Origins of Boys' Nicknames

Percent	Origin	Example
19%	Variation or short form of last name	Mort from Moriarty
8%	Physical characteristics	Torch ("Because I have red hair.")
3%	Initials	J.C. from first and last names
2%	Some connection with first name	Marko from Mark
2%	Sports ability	Night Train ("Because when I'm going in for a layup, I don't stop.")
2%	Indirect connection with last name	Tree from Pyne
1%	Clothes worn	Klopp from a name of jacket
1%	Sports figure	Cheesie ("Because I like Gerry Cheevers, the goalie for the Boston Bruins.")

List 13
The Origins of Boys' Nicknames *(continued)*

Percent	Origin	Example
1%	TV program character	Bodine from "Beverly Hillbillys"
1%	Musical ability	Johnny Lightning ("Because I play guitar and sing.")
1%	Newspaper cartoon figure	Zonker from Doonesbury cartoon strip ("Because my hair is similar to Zonker's)
1%	Name of previous school attended	Tucker from Tucker High School
1%	Father's first name	Little Richard ("Because I am like my father.")
1%	Personality or behavior	Turtle ("Because I walk slowly and casually.")
13%	No reason known to bearer of nickname	
45%	Do not have a nickname	

List 14
The Origins of Girls' Nicknames

Percent	Origin	Example
9%	Physical characteristics	Squirt ("Because I'm the youngest and the shortest.")
5%	Variation or short form of last name	Skee from Zaremski
4%	Initials	Tee from Tracy
3%	Personality or behavior	Dizzi ("Because of the things I do.")
3%	Some connection with first name	Katis from Katharine
3%	Nonsensical baby name	Baskoco ("Because when I was little they would ask me my name and I would say, 'Baskoco'.")
2%	TV program character	Charlie's Angel ("Because people say I look like Shelly Hack.")

List 14
The Origins of Girls' Nicknames *(continued)*

Percent	Origin	Example
1%	First and middle name	Beefy from Beth Ann
1%	Sports ability	Jenny Bug ("Because I liked to swim when I was younger.")
1%	Indirect connection with last name	Private Joke (rhymes with last name, Koch)
1%	Cooking ability	Dumb Italian ("Because I make good meatballs.")
1%	First, middle, and last name	(Nanny) Goat from Nancy Ann G.
6%	No reason known to bearer of nickname	
60%	Do not have a nickname	

names. No less than 19 percent of these boys had nicknames based on variations or short forms of their last names. Eight percent had nicknames derived from physical characteristics. For girls the two chief sources of nicknames were reversed. Physical characteristics ranked first and accounted for 9 percent. Variations of last names were responsible for 5 percent. The other boys' and girls' nicknames were drawn from diverse sources.

How well-liked are nicknames? All students rated their nicknames. I found that only 6 percent of the boys and 15 percent of the girls who possessed nicknames disliked them even to some degree, whereas 69 percent of the boys and 72 percent of the girls approved of their nicknames to at least a small extent. The remainder were indifferent.

The small percentages of students disliking their nicknames suggest that persons have substantial control over what they are called. Disliked nicknames should die from lack of response. However, if name bearers directly attack unwanted nicknames, they may only provoke further use, particularly if competition or conflict exists between the name-giver and the name-recipient as between siblings. For example, my sister-in-law, Suzanne, intensely disliked a childhood nickname, "Queen Suspot." But the stronger she reacted against it, the more gleefully her brother would chant it.

List 15
Nicknames Liked by Those Who Have Them

Boys	*Girls*
A.J.	A.V.
Bodine	Buzz
Cheesie	C.C. (Crazy Cat)
Clyde	Chicken
Gotz	Cricket
Pizon	Dee
Quack	Fergie
Seb	Frack
Sig	Goat
Squat	Nickerbockerbeets
Tone	Pecosa
Tucker	Shortcake
	Shorty
	Skee
	Squirt
	Tange
	Tee
	Whoopie

These names were given a top rating of 9 on a 1 to 9 scale.

List 16
Nicknames Disliked by Those Who Have Them

Boys	*Girls*
Leads	Beefy
Slyme	Burt
	Haaanegan
	Roxy
	Thatch

These names were given low ratings of 1, 2, or 3 on a 1 to 9 scale.

Lists 15 and 16 display nicknames that were highly liked or disliked. It is easy to understand why some names merit the disliked category. Names such as Slyme for boys and Beefy or Burt for girls are unlikely to endear themselves to their afflicted possessors.

On the other hand, it is surprising to find that boys can like nicknames such as Quack and Squat, or that girls like Chicken, Goat, Shorty, Squirt, and Whoopie. But they do. A nickname can be a sign of affection between friends, however repulsive it might be to others.

High variability characterizes the use of nicknames. One boy and five girls possessed nicknames that were used by only one other person. On the other extreme, six boys and six girls possessed nicknames that were used by everybody. Generally speaking, there are three types of nicknames: (1) those used only by friends and acquaintances, (2) those used only by family members, and (3) those used by family, friends, and acquaintances.

The large majority of nicknames were coined and used exclusively by friends and acquaintances. Very few students reported nickname usage by teachers, although students frequently do give nicknames to teachers. These are rarely, if ever, used in the teachers' presence.

If you're named Slyme or Beefy it is just as well that only your friends (?) use it.

8
A Family
of Nicknames

Joining the Fillipo family is similar to entering a religious order. The members assign all initiates a nickname, one often based on physical characteristics. From that day forward they are addressed by this nickname.

For the Fillipo clan, nicknames are an integral part of family membership. In contrast, the Schultzes act as if nicknames carried psoriasis. It's not that friends haven't tried to pin nicknames on the Schultz children. But the Schultz family, perhaps instinctively, knows that if a nickname is never acknowledged, it will not stick.

Unlike the Fillipo and Schultz families, nicknames occur sporadically in most households. For example, my family had only one nickname and it was owned by the third of my four sisters. As a baby, Caroline dissolved into laughter on hearing that well-loved nonsense phrase, "Ketcha-ketcha-koo." She became to one and all, Ketch.

A chart detailing the Fillipo family tree would show a pervasive use of nicknames. Muzzy and Loy are the grandparents. Muzzy is derived from the moustache which he proudly wears. Loy is a transformation of the mother's given name, Lorraine.

Spider, the eldest of six children, is named for his tall, thin physique. Spider married Joan, the only member of this clan who refuses to accept a nickname. Their oldest child is called Buck because of his running ability. The second son, Teen Angel, received his moniker because, during his early adolescence, he resembled nothing so much as a reincarnated fifties teenybopper. The third child, named James after the father, has been tagged, Jimbo. Their only girl, Diana, is known as Dina. The last child's name, Quinten, has been corrupted into Tin Man, a take-off on Dorothy's friend.

Muzzy and Loy's second child and only girl became Sis. She married Butch, who once wore this male hair style. They have three children: Norton, Brenda Starr, and Kevin Bender. Norton is named because he closely resembles Norton, the character played by Art Carney on the "Honeymooners." Brenda Starr acquired her nickname by simple association with her given name, Brenda. And Kevin picked up the "surname" Bender because of his ability as a contortionist.

Bob Steele is Muzzy's third child, named because that movie cowboy was his boyhood hero.

Twenty-five years after Steele last rode into the TV sunset, a namesake lives on. Bob Steele married Gretchen, a name unrelated to her real name. The origin of this label is unknown, but perhaps it is because she reflects certain Germanic stereotypes. Bob Steele and Gretchen have two daughters. The older appears to have been cloned from her father and thus is called Dad. The younger, Kathyrn, could not in her toddler years pronounce the short form of her name—"me Skate"—and so Skate she became.

Muzzy and Loy produced three other children. Happy Tooth has one funny-looking front tooth. Lenny, whose real name is Paul Henry, was nicknamed after his great grandfather whom he closely resembles. Lenny wed Lester, whose masculine nickname derives from her given name, Leslie. Lastly there is Roger Ramjet, named for his love of flying and his service in the U.S. Air Force. Roger married Sheribell—a take-off on her given name. They have a son called Just-in-Time, an alliteration on Justin.

These nicknames reveal the Fillipos to be an affectionate, fun loving, TV-watching family.

9
The Power of Names

How many Caesars and Pompeys . . . by mere inspiration of the names, have been rendered worthy of them? And how many . . . are there, who might have done exceedingly well in the world, had not their characteristics and spirits been totally depressed (by their names)?

—Laurence Sterne

Most of us don't share Sterne's determinism in its strong form. We realize that we can't create a great president by naming our first-born Abraham, or a conquering general by labeling him Napoleon.

I suspect, however, that most new parents subscribe to name determinism in its weak form. Consider the effort, and perhaps argument, which parents often devote to the choice of their baby's name. And prospective parents probably purchase a large percentage of best sellers such as *The Best Baby Name Book* and *What to Name Your Baby*.

WEE PALS by Morrie Turner. © King Features Syndicate 1973. Courtesy of Field Newspaper Syndicate

One believer in the power of first names is Dr. Wilbur Geoffrey Gaffney of the University of Nebraska. He has formulated two axioms about the power of names:

> Axiom I: "Men with extroverted, or 'he-man' names tend to become leaders in extroverted pursuits, such as the military life." Such names include Jack, Tom, Harry, Bud, Bob and Sam.
>
> Axiom II: "Children with unusual names tend to become bookish early in life, and (perhaps as a direct consequence) frequently end up as professors."

Gaffney expounds a position that is generally accepted by novelists, playwrights, scriptwriters, and others who concoct names. For example, the British writer Angus Wilson, talking about the characters Tom and Piers in his novel, *Setting the World on Fire,* said:

> Well, of course Tom and Piers represent the two sides of me. Part of me wants to take enormous risks, experiment with form, let my imagination rip, dazzle people. That's Piers. But then there's another part that says, "Steady on, the ice is beginning to crack." That's Tom. He stands for method and order and regularity.

Most of us hold stereotypes about Nathaniels, Joels, Taras and Jacquelines, to list a few names. These name stereotypes exercise their power to shape behavior by means of a process that psychologists call the self-fulfilling prophecy. It works like this:

Step 1: Most first names are accompanied by wide-ly-held stereotypes. For example, Danielle is stereotyped as beautiful, young, petite, intelligent, and French, while Betty is perceived as average, domestic, old fashioned, a typical housewife.

Step 2: When initially meeting people we imagine what they are like. We do this based upon their name stereotypes, as well as other characteristics, such as height and clothing.

Step 3: These rudimentary perceptions influence our behavior toward new acquaintances. If male, we are likely to treat Betty as if she were someone's mother, but to pursue Danielle as a possible girl friend.

Step 4: The other persons react to our treatment. Betty perceives us as friendly but sexually disinterested, while Danielle perceives us as a potential boy friend. Both Betty and Danielle then react to us consistent with their perceptions.

Step 5: Over time, the other persons' behavior

conforms more and more closely to that which we expect of them. Danielle pays more attention to her looks and her clothing and appears more beautiful as a result. In contrast, Betty concentrates on mastering domestic skills such as cooking and sewing, and becomes more proficient in these.

Next let us turn to some specific research findings related to first name effects.

PERSONAL POPULARITY

I asked about 1600 elementary school boys and girls to name the three boys and three girls in their class they liked best as well as the three they liked least. The most popular girls tended to have well-liked names. There were no clear relationships between the popularity of boys and their first names.

EDUCATIONAL ACHIEVEMENT AND IQ

Using the sample of elementary school students mentioned above, I found that girls' IQs and school achievement scores were related to first name popularity. Boys' IQ and achievement scores showed similar, but smaller, relationships.

EMOTIONAL MALADJUSTMENT

Unusual names have been linked to various types

of emotional disturbance in men. For example, a study of Harvard students found that the bearers of uncommon names flunked out in greater numbers and showed more neurotic behavior than students who bore common names.

Unusual names appear to be unrelated to emotional maladjustment in women, perhaps because women are much more likely to have unusual names.

10
Changing Your Name

The Babudja people of Zimbabwe believe that an habitually crying child possesses an inadequate name. The crying is thought to be a sign from the spirits that the name must be changed.

The Tiwi of Northern Australia are convinced that whenever a widow remarries all the personal names of her children become taboo. The new husband has the duty to give names to all of them regardless of their ages. In practice, however, renaming is limited to males under thirty-five and females not yet past early adolescence. Thus, since young Tiwi women generally marry much older men, Tiwi males may experience as many as four or five name changes.

First-name changing in cultures such as the Babudja and the Tiwi follows traditional customs, much as an American woman usually adopts her husband's last name upon marriage. But in America, nontraditional name changing often occurs when individuals dislike their own names.

To find out how widespread first name dissatisfaction is, I asked about two thousand students to say whether they liked, disliked, or felt neutral about their first names. Although 91 percent of the boys and 90 percent of the girls in second grade liked their names, these percentages fell in grade six to 77 and 58 percent. In grade 11, only 61 percent of the boys and 50 percent of the girls liked their names. Other studies show that the percentage of college students who like their names is slightly higher. But there remains a large reservoir of persons who might consider changing their first names.

You can't stretch yourself taller, you can't make your gray eyes blue, and the sunshine only brings out your freckles, but you do have the power to change your name. You can switch to your middle name with minimal hassle and no expense. Unfortunately, the dropped name may pop up at the darndest times because official records lurk forever in computer banks. Or you can legally change your name. Complete the forms, pay the fees, give public notice, and a judge will certify your new choice.

If you decide to adopt a new name, pick one that fits you. An active, dominant male might like Daniel, Joseph, or James, but not Aubrey or Joel. A sophisticated and formal young woman might choose Jacqueline or Vanessa, but never Dana, Peggy, or Mary Jo.

Change your name at one of life's breakpoints. As you begin college, leave home, or start a new job you'll meet new friends who won't know the old name exists. Parents, however, will have to be convinced that you're not repudiating them along with the name that seemed so perfect twenty years ago.

11
Practical Questions

How can we pick a suitable middle name for our child?

Middle names are a relatively recent innovation in the United States. Only three of the fifty-six signers of the Declaration of Independence—the two Lees from Virginia and Robert Treat Paine of Massachusetts—had middle names.

A middle name has several potential uses which should be considered before choosing one for your child. It aids in the identification of otherwise identically-named persons. This isn't important if you're named Fardislaw Gryzynski, but for the Jim Smiths of the world it makes a difference.

A well-selected middle name can also placate spouses and grandparents who argued for a subsequently rejected first name. For example, I thought Kim would be a beautiful first name for my oldest daughter, but my wife didn't. We compromised with Kathleen Kim.

Perhaps most importantly, a middle name can

replace a first name which has become disliked. One Canadian mother wrote that she gave each of her children "adventurous" first names—Gwendolen and Olivia for her daughters, Brecken and St. John for her boys, but that she was careful to choose popular second names to which they could switch.

Certain girls' names pop up frequently as middle names: Anne, Lynn, and Mary are three favorites, possibly because they blend well with many first names.

My husband and I cannot agree on a name for our future son. I detest his choice and he despises mine. How can we extricate ourselves from this impasse?

First, attempt to find a third name that is, if not beloved, at least satisfactory to both of you. However, if this approach fails, an appeal to the "Court of Last Resort" is needed. You flip a coin and your husband calls it, or vice versa. You may wish to have a witness or two present.

The two alternatives should be balanced as much as possible before the coin is tossed. For example, you might agree that the loser names the baby if it turns out to be a girl, or that the loser names the next child, or perhaps picks the boy's middle name.

Recognize, too, that unrelenting conflict over such a small item may be a sign of deeper problems in a marriage. Of course, your best hope is that the newborn will be a bonnie lassie.

How can I give my son an upper-class name?

Give him an Anglo-Saxon surname as a first name—Anderson, Burnham, and Thayer are good choices. Be aware though that an upper-class name without supporting credentials is likely to prove a burden. If however, you can provide him with a Princeton education, flawless teeth, and clothes by Halston and Bill Blass, maitre d's should greet him like the blueblood that his name suggests he is.

P.S. It would help if he marries a woman nicknamed Bunny, Bitsy, Buffy, or Muffy.

Do certain first names lead to nicknames?

Although many last names are readily transformed into nicknames—for example, Busse into Bus, there are few first names that lend themselves to true nicknames.

Parents who wish to avoid nicknames for their children might better be wary of initials. P.I.G., B.A.G., and R.A.T. are three that should be shunned.

Parents can also lessen the possibility of nicknames by refusing to name children after themselves. Such identical names often lead to nicknames for the younger person.

HAGAR THE HORRIBLE by Dik Browne. Reprinted by permission of King Features Syndicate, Inc.

My ten-year-old son came home yesterday and said he hates his name and wants to change it. What should I do?

Discuss the situation with him to determine how intense his hatred is, and how long he has felt this way.

If his hatred is longstanding—a year or more —and severe, together you and he should explore possibilities. Perhaps he wouldn't mind being called by his middle name. Maybe he would like a variation of his given name—for example, Chip or Chuck in place of Charles. Or—the least desirable alternative—you might help him choose another name. I heard from one man who was known as Chris even though his name was Gardner Joseph.

If your son's dislike is either newly minted or lacking intensity, insist that he endure his current name for another six months or so, after which you will discuss it again.

My wife's mother insists that our first son be named after her husband. What should we do?

Grandparents ought to be politely told to stop meddling. Naming is one of the small joys of parenthood, and should be jealously defended against encroachment.

It is conceivable that you and your wife together will repeat his name 100,000 times during the next twenty years. If the name is disliked, each use will recall the unfortunate decision you once made. Moreover, if you don't like the name, your son probably won't either.

On the other hand, if you and your wife really like your father-in-law's name, go ahead and use it. You'll strengthen family ties, while also creating some name confusion. But don't mistake liking your father-in-law for liking your father-in-law's name.

12
Intriguing Questions

Why do women seem to be more concerned with first names than are men?

Women are more concerned than men with how they present themselves to other people. For example, women place greater emphasis on clothing, hair color, eye makeup, and perfumes. It follows that women should be especially concerned about first names because they are an important factor in any initial presentation of self. This concern has led many women to alter the spelling of their first names. For example, President Johnson's two daughters, Luci and Lynda, exchanged vowels.

Women also have greater cause to be concerned with first names because their given name is probably the only one they will use throughout life.

Do Americans prefer the long or short form of names?

Many male names possess both a short name

and an "ee" name. For example, William has both Bill and Willie.

Short male names are generally preferred over both the formal name and the "ee" name. Thus Tom is preferred over Thomas and Tommy by wide margins. There are exceptions. Daniel is selected before both Dan and Danny, and Ronald is the choice over Ron and Ronnie. Ronald Reagan, are you listening?

The short forms generally have a masculine flavor, while the "ee" names are often perceived as feminine or childish. Most males shuck their "ee" names upon reaching the teenage years, although converting mothers and grandmothers may prove difficult. In the American South, however, an "ee" name may be retained—for example, Jimmy Carter, Willie Nelson. Often sports figures too are known by an "ee" name—Willie Mays, Johnny Bench, Jimmy Brown.

Very few girls' names have both a short and an "ee" name, but there are exceptions (Elizabeth, Beth, Betty). Some female names have "ee" forms which are used in all but the most formal situations—Judy, Cindy, Lucy, Peggy. These "ee" forms are often given at birth. There are no clear popularity differences among the three forms.

How quickly do names move in and out of fashion?

The most common male names in the American colonies at the time of the Revolution were John, William, George, and Thomas. Then came Richard, Robert, Philip, James and Charles. Four of these—John, Thomas, Robert, and James—are among the 20 currently best-liked boys' names. The other six names are not unknown today.

Lists of women's names in the colonial period are scarce. A name count of women who were married in one Virginia county in the years 1772-1800 produced the following top ten: Elizabeth, Mary, Sarah, Ann, Nancy, Sally, Lucy, Susanna, Frances, and Betsy.

Only Nancy makes the current list of 20 most popular names. Most of the remaining names are given occasionally today, but only Elizabeth, Mary, and Ann occur with frequency. Moreover, Sarah is currently making a comeback.

These comparisons with colonial names demonstrate that male name popularity changes very slowly. In the twentieth century David, Michael, and Christopher have risen, while Edward, Louis, and more recently George, have fallen. Most male names have remained popular or unpopular, as the case might be.

Female names show much greater changes. Only Mary has retained high popularity throughout this century. Frances, Ruth, and Margaret have declined steeply, while previous unknowns— Michelle, Jill, and Dawn—are now "in."

Why is it that some persons don't like their names?

Perhaps because they don't like themselves. Dislike for one's own name may reflect an otherwise concealed case of low self-esteem.

People may not like their names because the ones they bear are generally disliked. There is a much greater chance that Edith will dislike her name than that Michelle will. Ditto for Schuyler and David.

Paradoxically, some persons dislike their names because they are too unusual, while others dislike their names because they are too common. Still others dislike their names because of the way they sound.

I have heard that teachers give higher grades to students with more popular names. Is this accurate?

In a now well-known study psychologists Herbert Harari and John McDavid related first name stereotypes to grading practices. Four popular names (David, Michael, Lisa, Karen) and four unpopular names (Elmer, Hubert, Adelle, Bertha) were randomly assigned to essays written by elementary school students. The essays with popular first names were generally given higher grades by women elementary teachers than were essays with unpopular names. The name Adelle, however, was an exception: essays bearing this name were graded higher than those assigned the more popular names, Lisa and Karen.

Louisa Seraydarian and I did a similar study using undergraduate teacher education students. However, we found that grades assigned to children's essays were unaffected by the children's first names.

The Harari and McDavid results are provocative, but there is a possibility that vague grading standards contributed to their finding that first names have an effect on grading.

Is it true that American Blacks are more imaginative than whites in their name selections?

Yes. Although most American Blacks now give the same first names as other Americans, a minority still chooses highly unusual and often romantic names. One authority on Black names, P. Robert Paustian, has traced this naming tradition back to "the African practice of giving the most unique names possible and attaching considerable prestige to the most memorable."

Geographical place names are one source of unusual Black names. In 1981, there were, for example, 12 Kenyas born in Pennsylvania. Blacks have also been named Nigeria, Asia Minor, Arabia, and London.

The Bible serves as a reservoir of Black names—De Word of God, Queen Esther, Delilah, and Hosannah. Romantic classics are sometimes tapped for names such as Lancelot, Rowena, Guinevere, and Ophelia.

African names are another source of Black names—Kwame, Ayesha, Rashad, Jamil, and Kenyatta. The television spectacular, "Roots," has presumably contributed to an upsurge in the use of African names. Little Kuntas and Kizzys memorialize this program.

Other Black names seem to have been created by the parents. Consider Clendolia, Pernella, Lunelle, Wildetta, and Deodolphus.

Why do actors, actresses, and writers often change their names?

They wish to put forth an image different from that projected by their real names. Moreover, they may change names in order to disguise their religion, ethnic group, or sex.

Actors and actresses routinely take stage names. Most choose a popular first name and couple it with an Anglo-Saxon surname. Marion Morrison became John Wayne, Nathan Birnbaum changed to George Burns, and Frances Gumm metamorphosed into Judy Garland. Other show business types capitalize on the unforgetableness of unusual names. Rip Torn, Gale Storm, Soupy

Sales, Chevy Chase, and Groucho Marx are several who have used this approach.

Two renowned novelists, George Eliot and George Sand, were women who adopted a man's name to avoid nineteenth century prejudice against female writers. A reverse prejudice exists today in one literary sphere: Almost all Gothic novels list female authors, even when written by men.

How do novelists select names for their characters?

Serious writers choose names for their fictional characters with exacting care. Henry James, for example, believed that "it is often enough to damn a well-intentioned story, that the heroine should be called Kate rather than Katherine; the hero Anthony rather than Ernest."

Creative writers recognize that names are surrounded by stereotypes which can anchor the personality of a fictional character. Dickens used names most effectively to shape his characters. Ebenezer (Scrooge) is obviously an odd fellow; Bob (Cratchit), a regular guy; and Uriah (Heep), a confirmed weirdo. Shakespeare, too, sometimes selected names which defined his characters. Falstaff just has to be a comic character, while Shylock is obviously a villain.

Numerous modern writers including William Faulkner, F. Scott Fitzgerald, and William Styron are also known for their skillful choice of names.

Appendix A
Popularity Ratings of
Boys' Names

All names are rated from 1 to 10, with each rating being given to 10 percent of the boys' names. Thus a 10 means that a name is in the top 10 percent in likability of all boys' names. A 9 places a name in the second 10 percent. And so on down to a rating of 1, which indicates that a name is in the bottom 10 percent in likability.

In general, 9 and 10 indicate well liked names; 3 through 8 signify average popularity; and 1 and 2 indicate disliked names.

The ratings for these 179 names are taken from my most recent research.

Name	Rating	Name	Rating
Adam	8	Armin	1
Alan	9	Arnold	2
Albert	5	Arthur	4
Alfred	2	Aubrey	5
Altair	1	Barry	8
Andrew	9	Bartholomew	1
Angelo	6	Bela	1
Anthony	10	Benjamin	8
Archie	2	Bernard	5

Bradford	5	Douglas	8
Bradley	6	Dwayne	8
Brent	5		
Brian	10	Dwight	5
Brooke	6	Earl	3
Bruce	9	Edward	7
		Edwin	2
Calvin	3	Eric	10
Cameron	7	Eugene	3
Carl	7		
Carlin	3	Faber	1
Carlton	5	Florian	1
Chad	7	Ford	1
		Francis	5
Charles	8	Frank	7
Christopher	10	Frederick	4
Clarence	2		
Claude	2	Gardner	3
Clifford	7	Garret	4
Conrad	5	Gary	10
		George	7
Courtney	3	Gerard	2
Craig	9	Glenn	8
Curt	8		
Curtis	7	Grant	6
Dale	6	Gregory	9
Dallas	5	Grier	1
		Guy	4
Dana	4	Gwyn	2
Daniel	10	Harold	3
Darius	2		
David	10	Harry	4
Dean	8	Harvey	2
Dennis	7	Herbert	2
		Howard	4
Dino	6	Hugh	3
Dirk	2	Ian	6
Dixon	2		
Donald	7	Ingmar	1

James	10	Maurice	7
Jan	3	Melvin	1
Jay	9	Michael	10
Jayce	2	Montgomery	3
Jefferson	4	Nathan	7
Jeffrey	9	Nathaniel	7
Jerald	5	Neil	9
Jerome	6		
Joel	8	Nicholas	9
John	10	Norman	2
Jonathan	10	Nunzio	4
		Otto	4
Joseph	10	Patrick	8
Keith	10	Paul	9
Kenneth	8		
Kerry	5	Peter	9
Kevin	10	Philip	9
Khalig	1	Rajiv	1
		Ralph	4
Kirk	8	Randall	6
Kristian	3	Raymond	7
Lamar	4		
Lawrence	5	Richard	9
Lee	8	Robert	9
Leonard	3	Robin	4
		Rocco	2
Les	5	Rodney	4
Lester	3	Roger	7
Lex	3		
Louis	6	Ronald	6
Lyman	1	Ross	4
Malig	1	Rudy	6
		Russell	6
Mark	10	Salvatore	4
Marshall	4	Samuel	7
Martin	6		
Marvin	2	Schuyler	1
Matthew	9	Scott	10

Shawn	9	Thomas	10
Sheldon	5	Timothy	9
Skipper	3		
Spencer	5	Todd	7
		Toro	2
Stanley	3	Tracey	1
Stanton	2	Tyler	7
Stephen	10	Victor	6
Sterling	3	Vincent	8
Stockton	5		
Stuart	8		
		Wade	6
Sumner	1	Walter	6
Teran	4	Warren	6
Terrance	5	Wayne	8
Terry	8	William	9

Appendix B
Popularity Ratings of Girls' Names

All names are rated from 1 to 10, with each rating being given to 10 percent of the girls' names. Thus a 10 means that a name is in the top 10 percent in likability of all girls' names. A 9 places a name in the second 10 percent. And so on down to a rating of 1 which indicates that a name is in the bottom 10 percent in likability.

In general, 9 and 10 indicate well liked names; 3 through 8 signify average popularity; and 1 and 2 indicate disliked names.

The ratings for these 246 names are taken from my most recent research.

Adrian	7	Anne	8
Alesia	4	Annette	8
Alizon	3	Arlene	4
Allison	4		
Amy	8	Audrey	5
Andrea	10	Barbara	10
		Bernice	1
Angele	7	Beth	8
Anita	6	Beth Ann	3
Anna	5	Betsy	9

Betty	2	Deanna	7
Beverly	4	Deborah	8
Birgit	8		
Bonita	1	Debra	8
Bonnie	4	Denise	9
Brenda	3	Diana	8
		Diane	9
Bunny	3	Dina	6
Candace	5	Dolores	2
Carmella	5		
Carmen	5	Donna	8
Carol	8	Doranne	2
Carolyn	8	Doreen	4
		Dorothea	1
Carrie	6	Dylin	2
Cassandra	4	Edith	1
Catherine	9		
Cecilia	4	Eileen	6
Celeste	5	Elaine	6
Charlotte	4	Eleanor	2
		Elizabeth	8
Cheryl	10	Ella Mae	1
Christina	10	Ellen	9
Christine	10		
Cindy	9	Emily	2
Claire	3	Erica	7
Claudette	3	Eveann	1
		Felica	1
Colette	6	Florence	1
Constance	3	Frances	3
Crickett	3		
Cynthia	7	Francine	3
Dana	10	Gail	5
Danielle	10	Georgiana	2
		Gillian	2
Danita	4	Gina	7
Darlene	7	Ginger	7
Darryl	3		
Dawn	10	Gloria	4

Grace	5	Karla	7
Gretchen	5		
Gwen	6	Kate	9
Hallie	2	Kathleen	9
Heather	9	Kathryn	9
		Kay	7
Helen	4	Kelly	9
Hilary	2	Kimberly	8
Holly	6		
Hope	5	Kristen	9
Irene	2	Kristi	10
Isabella	1	Kristiana	9
		Laura	9
Jacqueline	10	Lee	7
Jane	5	Leishia	3
Janene	7		
Janet	8	Leona	3
Janice	9	Leslie	9
Jeanette	6	Leta	6
		Linda	10
Jeanne	6	Lindy	5
Jennifer	10	Lisa	10
Jenny	9		
Jeri Ann	1	Lois	3
Jill	10	Lola May	1
Joan	6	Loretta	4
		Lori	9
Joanne	9	Lorraine	6
Jodie	5	Lou Ann	2
Johanna	3		
Joy	6	Lucinda	1
Joyce	6	Lurene	2
Juanita	3	Lydia	4
		Lynn	10
Judith	5	Marcia	6
Julia	8	Marcie	6
Justine	4		
Karen	10	Margaret	4
Kari	7	Marguerite	5

Name		Name	
Maria	9	Paula	6
Marianne	7	Pauline	5
Marilyn	6	Peggy	4
Marina	5	Penny	3
		Phoebe	2
Marion	3	Randy	6
Marjorie	2		
Marlissa	4	Rebecca	7
Martha	2	Regina	6
Mary	8	Renee	10
Mary Elizabeth	3	Risa	2
		Rita	4
Mary Ellen	5	Roberta	2
Mary Helen	1		
Mary Jo	2	Robin	10
Mary Kay	2	Rochelle	8
Mary Lynn	3	Rosalie	3
Marysia	2	Rose	7
		Rose Ann	5
Maureen	7	Rosemarie	6
Megan	6		
Melanie	4	Rosemary	6
Melinda	5	Rosemede	1
Melissa	9	Rosina	4
Melody	3	Ruth	3
		Sally	7
Merry	4	Sandra	8
Meta	1		
Michelle	10	Sara	8
Monika	8	Sharon	9
Myra	1	Sheila	7
Nancy	10	Shelda	1
		Shelly	5
Nanette	4	Sherry	7
Nicole	10		
Nina	6	Shirl	4
Noreen	2	Shirlene	3
Pamela	8	Shobhana	1
Patricia	9	Simone	1

Stacey	7	Valerie	8
Stephanie	10		
		Valli	2
Susan	10	Vanessa	8
Suzanne	10	Vaughan	2
Tammy	7	Vickie	10
Tara	8	Victoria	5
Temperance	1	Vivian	5
Terry	9		
		Wanda	1
Theresa	9	Watonah	1
Tina	7	Wendy	7
Towanda	1	Yolanda	1
Tracy	8	Yvette	5
Tuesday	5	Yvonne	7

Sources of Quotations

CHAPTER 2

"A rose by any other name . . . " William Shakespeare, *Romeo and Juliet,* Act II, Scene 2, Line 43.

CHAPTER 5

"I have a right to speak . . . " Henry James quoted in L. Edel, *Henry James, the untried years: 1843–1870.* Philadelphia: Lippincott, 1953. Page 56.

"My oldest brother's name . . . " Letter printed in Ann Landers' column, *Philadelphia Inquirer,* January 25, 1978. Page 2E.

"that they had about run out of girls' names . . . " James O. Palmer, *The psychological assessment of children.* New York: Wiley, 1970. Page 34.

CHAPTER 7

"All my life I have been called Shorty . . . " Personal letter to me, dated May 26, 1976.

CHAPTER 9

"How many Caesars and Pompeys . . . " Laurence Sterne, *The life and opinions of Tristram Shandy.* New York: Liveright Publishing Company, 1925. Page 39.

Axioms I and II. W.G. Gaffney, Tell me your name and your business; or, some considerations upon the purposeful naming of children. *Names*, 1971, 19, pages 37 and 39.

"Well, of course Tom and Piers . . . " Angus Wilson quoted in Michael Barber, A talk with Angus Wilson. *New York Times Book Review*, November 16, 1980. Page 41.

CHAPTER 12

"It is often enough to damn a well-intentioned story . . . " Henry James, *Notes and reviews*. Cambridge, Mass.: Dunster House, 1921. Page 4.

"the African practice of giving the most unique names . . . " P.R. Paustian, The evolution of personal naming practices among American Blacks. *Names*, 1978, 26, page 187.

References

CHAPTER 1: LABELING

Arthaud, R. L., Hohneck, A. N., Ramsey, C. H., and Pratt, K. C. The relation of family name preferences to their frequency in the culture. *Journal of Social Psychology,* 1948, 28, 19-37.

Broom, L., Beem, H. P., and Harris, V. Characteristics of 1,107 petitioners for change of name. *American Sociological Review,* 1955, 20, 33-39.

Hartman, A. A. Name styles in relation to personality. *Journal of General Psychology,* 1958, 59, 289-294.

Lawson, E. D. Men's first names, nicknames, and short names: A semantic differential analysis. *Names,* 1973, 21, 22-27.

Schoenfeld, N. An experimental study of some problems relating to stereotypes. *Archives of Psychology,* 1942, 38, No. 270, 1-57.

Shearer, L. What's in a name. *The Sunday Bulletin/Parade Magazine,* October 14, 1973, page 4.

Wells, F. L. & Palwick, H. R. Notes on usage of male personal names. *Journal of Social Psychology,* 1950, 31, 291-294.

Zweigenhaft, R. Name styles in America and name styles in New Zealand. *Journal of Social Psychology,* 1975, 97, 289-290.

CHAPTER 2: THE POPULARITY OF FIRST NAMES

Cumming, E. The name is the message. *Transaction,* July/August, 1967, 4, 50-52.

Marcus, M. G. The power of a name. *Psychology Today,* 1976, 10, 75-76 ff.

CHAPTER 3: THE RISE AND FALL OF NAMES

Buchanan, B. A. and Bruning, J. L. Connotative meanings of first names and nicknames on three dimensions. *Journal of Social Psychology*, 1971, 85, 143-144.

Lawson, E. D. Men's first names, nicknames, and short names: A semantic differential analysis. *Names*, 1973, 21, 22-27.

Lawson, E. D. Women's first names: A semantic differential analysis. *Names*, 1974, 22, 52-58.

Schoenfeld, N. An experimental study of some problems relating to stereotypes. *Archives of Psychology*, 1942, 38, No. 270, 1-57.

Walton, W. E. The affective value of first names. *Journal of Applied Psychology*, 1937, 21, 396-409.

CHAPTER 4: CHOOSING A NAME

Brender, M. Some hypotheses about the psychodynamic significance of infant name selection. *Names*, 1963, 11, 1-9.

Busse, T. V., Busse, K. & Busse, M. Identical first names for parent and child. *Journal of Social Psychology*, 1979, 107, 293-294.

Drosdowski, G. *Lexikon der Vornamen*. Mannheim, West Germany: Dudenverlag, 1974.

Ecenbarger, W. Jane plays 2nd fiddle to Jennifer. *Philadelphia Inquirer*, February 16, 1976.

Jahoda, G. A note on Ashanti names and their relationship to personality. *British Journal of Psychology*, 1954, 45, 192-195.

Junghare, I. Y. Socio-psychological aspects and linguistic analysis of Marathi names. *Names*, 1975, 23, 31-43.

Miller, N. Some aspects of the name in culture-history. *American Journal of Sociology*, 1926-27, 32, 585-600.

Paustian, P. R. The evolution of personal naming practices among American Blacks. *Names*, 1978, 26, 177-191.

Price, R. & Price, S. Saramaka onomastics: An Afro-American naming system. *Ethology*, 1972, 11, 341-367.

Rennick, R. M. The Nazi name decrees of the nineteen thirties. *Names*, 1970, 18, 65-88.

Rossi, A. S. Naming children in middle-class families. *American Sociological Review*, 1965, 30, 499-513.

Tavuchis, N. Naming patterns and kinship among Greeks. *Ethnos*, 1971, 36, 152-162.

Tomasson, R. F. The continuity of Icelandic names and naming patterns. *Names*, 1975, 23, 281-289.

Weeks, T. E. Child-naming customs among the Yakima Indians. *Names*, 1971, 19, 252-256.

Wieschhoff, H. Names and naming customs among the Mashona in Southern Rhodesia. *American Anthropologist*, 1937, 39, 497-503.

CHAPTER 5: CHOOSING A NAME: BITS AND PIECES

JUNIORS

Busse, T. V., Busse, K. & Busse, M. Identical first names for parent and child. *Journal of Social Psychology*, 1979, 107, 293-294.

Plank, R. The use of "Jr." in relation to psychiatric treatment. *Names*, 1971, 19, 132-136.

SEX AND NAMES

Bruning, J. L. & Albott, W. Funny, you don't look Cecil. *Human Behavior*, 1974, 3, 56-57.

Eagleson, O. W. Students' reactions to their given-names. *Journal of Social Psychology*, 1946, 23, 187-195.

Ecenbarger, W. Jane plays 2nd fiddle to Jennifer. *Philadelphia Inquirer*, February 16, 1976.

ALLITERATIVE NAMES

Duckett, E. S. *Alfred the Great*. Chicago: University of Chicago Press, 1956.

Tomasson, R. F. The continuity of Icelandic names and naming patterns. *Names*, 1975, 23, 281-289.

CHAPTER 6: UNUSUAL NAMES

Bruning, J. L. The effects of connotative meaning on the learning of names. *Journal of Social Psychology*, 1972, 86, 105–110.

Busse, T. V. & Seraydarian, L. Frequency and desirability of first names. *Journal of Social Psychology*, 1978, 104, 143–144.

Chappell, N. C. Negro names. *American Speech*, 1929, 4, 272–275.

Dell, J. Sports people. *Philadelphia Inquirer*, March 13, 1981.

Eagleson, O. W. & Clifford, A. D. A comparative study of the names of white and Negro women college students. *Journal of Social Psychology*, 1945, 21, 57–64.

Ecenbarger, W. Everything but whatsisname. *Philadelphia Inquirer*, May 29, 1979.

Ellis, A. & Beechley, R. M. Emotional disturbance in children with peculiar given names. *Journal of Genetic Psychology*, 1954, 85, 337–339.

Gaffney, W. G. Tell me your name and your business; or, some considerations upon the purposeful naming of children. *Names*, 1971, 19, 34–42.

Hartman, A. A., Nicolay, R. C., & Hurley, J. Unique personal names as a social adjustment factor. *Journal of Social Psychology*, 1968, 75, 107–110.

Holmes, U. T. A study in Negro onomastics. *American Speech*, 1930, 5, 463–467.

Houston, T. J. & Sumner, F. C. Measurement of neurotic tendency in women with uncommon given names. *Journal of General Psychology*, 1948, 39, 289–292.

Keegan, A. From those folks in Iowa, a fan club for Bambi who? *Philadelphia Inquirer*, April 8, 1978.

Newman, E. *Strictly speaking*. Indianapolis: Bobbs-Merrill, 1974.

Paustian, P. R. The evolution of personal naming practices among American Blacks. *Names*, 1978, 26, 177–191.

Plottke, P. The child and his name. *Individual Psychology Bulletin*, 1950, 8, 150-157.

Savage, B. M. & Wells, F. L. A note on singularity in given names. *Journal of Social Psychology*, 1948, 27, 271-272.

Sherif, M. & Cantril, H. *The psychology of ego-involvements*. New York: Wiley, 1947.

Strunk, O. Attitudes toward one's name and one's self. *Journal of Individual Psychology*, 1958, 14, 64-67.

Zweigenhaft, R. L. The other side of unusual first names. *Journal of Social Psychology*, 1977, 103, 291-302.

CHAPTER 7: NICKNAMES

Morgan, J., O'Neill, C. & Harré, R. *Nicknames: Their origins and social consequences*. London: Routledge and Kegan Paul, 1979.

CHAPTER 9: THE POWER OF NAMES

Adelson, D. Attitudes toward first names: An investigation of the relation between self-acceptance, self-identity and group and individual attitudes toward first names (Doctoral dissertation, Columbia University, 1957). *Dissertation Abstracts*, 1957, 17, 1831. (University Microfilms No. 57-2945)

Blain, M. J. & Ramirez, M. Increasing sociometric rank, meaningfulness, and discriminability of children's names through reinforcement and interaction. *Child Development*, 1968, 39, 949-955.

Boshier, R. Self esteem and first names in children. *Psychological Reports*, 1968, 22, 762.

Bruning, J. L. & Albott, W. Funny, you don't look Cecil. *Human Behavior*, 1974, 3, 56-57.

Busse, T. V. First names, achievement, and IQ. Paper presented at the annual meeting of the Eastern Psychological Association, Washington, D.C., 1973.

Busse, T. V. & Seraydarian, L. The relationships between

first name desirability and school readiness, IQ, and school achievement. *Psychology in the Schools,* 1978, 15, 297-302.

Busse, T. V. & Seraydarian, L. First names and popularity in grade school children. *Psychology in the Schools,* 1979, 16, 149-153.

Ellis, A. & Beechley, R. M. Emotional disturbance in children with peculiar given names. *Journal of Genetic Psychology,* 1954, 85, 337-339.

Feldman, H. The problem of personal names as a universal element in culture. *American Imago,* 1959, 16, 237-250.

Flugel, I. On the significance of names. *British Journal of Medical Psychology,* 1930, 10, 208-213.

Gaffney, W. G. Tell me your name and your business; or, some considerations upon the purposeful naming of children. *Names,* 1971, 19, 34-42.

Garwood, S. G. First-name stereotypes as a factor in self-concept and school achievement. *Journal of Educational Psychology,* 1976, 68, 482-487.

Hartman, A. A., Nicolay, R. C., & Hurley, J. Unique personal names as a social adjustment factor. *Journal of Social Psychology,* 1968, 75, 107-110.

Houston, T. J. & Sumner, F. C. Measurement of neurotic tendency in women with uncommon given names. *Journal of General Psychology,* 1948, 39, 289-292.

Jahoda, G. A note on Ashanti names and their relationship to personality. *British Journal of Psychology,* 1954, 45, 192-195.

McDavid, J. W. and Harari, H. Stereotyping of names and popularity in grade-school children. *Child Development,* 1966, 37, 453-459.

Nelson, S. D. First-name stereotypes and expected academic achievement of students. *Psychological Reports,* 1977, 41, 1343-1344.

Plottke, P. On the psychology of proper names. *Individual Psychology Bulletin,* 1946, 5, 106-111.

Savage, B. M. & Wells, F. L. A note on singularity in given names. *Journal of Social Psychology*, 1948, 27, 271-272.

Strunk, O. Attitudes toward one's name and one's self. *Journal of Individual Psychology*, 1958, 14, 64-67.

Zweigenhaft, R. L. The other side of unusual first names. *Journal of Social Psychology*, 1977, 103, 291-302.

CHAPTER 10: CHANGING YOUR NAME

Adelson, D. Attitudes toward first names: An investigation of the relation between self-acceptance, self-identity and group and individual attitudes toward first names (Doctoral dissertation, Columbia University, 1957). *Dissertation Abstracts*, 1957, 17, 1831. (University Microfilms No. 57-2945)

Allen, L., Brown, V., Dickinson, L. & Pratt, K. C. The relation of first name preferences to their frequency in the culture. *Journal of Social Psychology*, 1941, 14, 279-293.

Ashley, L. R. N. Changing times and changing names: Reasons, regulations, and rights. *Names*, 1971, 19, 167-187.

Busse, T. V. Entwicklungsänderungen in der Vorliebe für den eigenen Vornamen (Developmental changes in liking one's own first name). *Zeitschrift für Entwicklungspsychologie und Pädagogische Psychologie*, 1980, 12, 213-216.

Eagleson, O. W. Students' reactions to their given-names. *Journal of Social Psychology*, 1946, 23, 187-195.

Falk, A. Identity and name changes. *Psychoanalytic Review*, 1975-76, 62, 647-657.

Hart, C. W. M. and Pilling, A. R. *The Tiwi of North Australia*. New York: Holt, Rinehart and Winston, 1960.

Lawson, E. D. Semantic differential analysis of men's first names. *Journal of Psychology*, 1971, 78, 229-240.

Murphy, W. F. A note on the significance of names. *Psychoanalytic Quarterly*, 1957, 26, 91-106.

Strunk, O. Attitudes toward one's name and one's self. *Journal of Individual Psychology*, 1958, 14, 64–67.

Wieschhoff, H. Names and naming customs among the Mashona in Southern Rhodesia. *American Anthropologist*, 1937, 39, 497–503.

CHAPTER 11: PRACTICAL QUESTIONS

MIDDLE NAMES

Randel, W. P. *The American Revolution: Mirror of a people.* Maplewood, New Jersey: Hamond, 1973.

UPPER-CLASS NAMES

Zweigenhaft, R. L. The other side of unusual first names. *Journal of Social Psychology*, 1977, 103, 291–302.

CHAPTER 12: INTRIGUING QUESTIONS

Do Americans prefer the long or short form of names?

Finch, M., Kilgren, H. & Pratt, K. C. The relation of first name preferences to age of judges or to different although overlapping generations. *Journal of Social Psychology*, 1944, 20, 249–264.

Lawson, E. D. Men's first names, nicknames, and short names: A semantic differential analysis. *Names*, 1973, 21, 22–27.

Van Buren, H. The American way with names. In R.W. Brislin (Ed.), *Topics in cultural learning*, Volume 2. Honolulu, Hawaii: East-West Center, University of Hawaii, 1974. (ERIC Document Reproduction Service No. ED 097 256)

How quickly do names move in and out of fashion?

Buchanan, B. A. and Bruning, J. L. Connotative meanings of first names and nicknames on three dimensions. *Journal of Social Psychology*, 1971, 85, 143-144.

Randel, W. P. *The American Revolution: Mirror of a people.* Maplewood, New Jersey: Hamond, 1973.

Stewart, G. R. *American given names.* New York: Oxford University Press, 1979.

Walton, W. E. The affective value of first names. *Journal of Applied Psychology,* 1937, 21, 396-409.

Why is it that some persons don't like their names?

Adelson, D. Attitudes toward first names: An investigation of the relation between self-acceptance, self-identity and group and individual attitudes toward first names (Doctoral dissertation, Columbia University, 1957). *Dissertation Abstracts,* 1957, 17, 1831. (University Microfilms No 57-2945)

Boshier, R. Self esteem and first names in children. *Psychological Reports,* 1968, 22, 762.

I have heard that teachers give higher grades to students with more popular names. Is this accurate?

Harari, H. & McDavid, J. W. Name stereotypes and teachers' expectations. *Journal of Educational Psychology,* 1973, 65, 222-225.

Seraydarian, L. & Busse, T. V. First-name stereotypes and essay grading. *Journal of Psychology,* 1981, 108, 253-257.

Is it true that American Blacks are more imaginative than whites in their name selections?

Busse, T. V. & Seraydarian, L. Desirability of first names, ethnicity and parental education. *Psychological Reports,* 1977, 40, 739-742.

Chappell, N. C. Negro names. *American Speech,* 1929, 4, 272-275.

Eagleson, O. W. & Clifford, A. D. A comparative study of the names of white and Negro women college students. *Journal of Social Psychology,* 1945, 21, 57-64.

Ecenbarger, W. Everything but whatsisname. *Philadelphia Inquirer,* May 29, 1979.

Gaither, F. Fanciful are Negro names. *New York Times Magazine,* February 10, 1929, page 19.

Holmes, U. T. A study in Negro onomastics. *American Speech*, 1930, 5, 463-467.

Loeb, V. So much for tradition. *Philadelphia Inquirer*, June 25, 1981.

Paustian, P. R. The evolution of personal naming practices among American Blacks. *Names*, 1978, 26, 177-191.

Why do actors, actresses, and writers often change their names?

Andersen, C. P. *The name game*. New York: Simon and Schuster, 1977.

Our Town. *Today Magazine/Philadelphia Inquirer*, March 4, 1979.

How do novelists select names for their characters?

Gale, R. L. Names in James. *Names*, 1966, 14, 83-108.

Terrell, D. Names and the nihilistic mood in *The Sound and the Fury*. In F. Tarpley (Ed.), *Labeled for life*. Commerce, Texas: Names Institute Press, 1977.

Welsh, C. *Character portraits from Dickens*. London: Chatto and Windus, 1908. Reprinted by Haskell House Publishers, New York, 1972.

Articles and Papers on First Names by Professor Busse

1. With Craig Love. The effect of first names on conflicted decisions: An experimental study. *Journal of Psychology*, 1973, 84, 253-256.
2. First names, achievement, and IQ. Paper presented at the annual meeting of the Eastern Psychological Association, Washington, D.C., 1973.
3. With James Helfrich. Changes in first name popularity across grades. *Journal of Psychology*, 1975, 89, 281-283.
4. With Louisa Seraydarian. Desirability of first names, ethnicity and parental education. *Psychological Reports*, 1977, 40, 739-742.
5. With Louisa Seraydarian. Frequency and desirability of first names. *Journal of Social Psychology*, 1978, 104, 143-144.
6. With Louisa Seraydarian. The relationships between first name desirability and school readiness, IQ, and school achievement. *Psychology in the Schools*, 1978, 15, 297-302.
7. With Louisa Seraydarian. First names and popularity in grade school children. *Psychology in the Schools*, 1979, 16, 149-153.
8. With Kathleen and Michael Busse. Identical first names for parent and child. *Journal of Social Psychology*, 1979, 107, 293-294.
9. Entwicklungsänderungen in der Vorliebe für den eigenen Vornamen (Developmental changes in liking one's

own first name). *Zeitschrift für Entwicklungspsychologie und Pädagogische Psychologie,* 1980, 12, 213–216.

10. With Louisa Seraydarian. First-name stereotypes and essay grading. *Journal of Psychology,* 1981, 108, 253–257.

11. Nickname usage in an American high school. *Names,* 1983, 31, in press.

If you know an unusual story about first names or nicknames that you would like to share, please send it to:

Dr. Thomas V. Busse
c/o The Green Ball Press
Post Office Box 29771
Elkins Park, Pa. 19117

I would enjoy hearing from you.

Additional copies of this book are available from:
The Green Ball Press
Dept. B
P.O. Box 29771
Elkins Park, Pa. 19117